10'08

BACK TO BASICS

The Back to Basics series was devised and produced by McRae Books Srl, Borgo S. Croce, 8, Florence (Italy)

Publishers: Anne McRae and Marco Nardi
Text: Anita Ganeri
Main Illustrations: Fiammetta Dogi
Other Illustrations: Antonella Pastorelli, Studio Stalio (Alessandro Cantucci, Fabiano Fabbrucci,)
Design: Marco Nardi
Layout: Nick Leggett (Starry Dog Books)
Color separations: Fotolito Toscana, Firenze

Library of Congress Cataloging-in-Publication Data

Ganeri, Anita, 1961-
  Dinosaurs / by Anita Ganeri.
      p. cm. -- (Back to basics)
  Includes index.
  ISBN 978-8860980489 (alk. paper)
  1. Dinosaurs. I. Title.
  QE861.4.G36 2007
  567.9--dc22
                                              2007007794

Printed and bound in Malaysia

BACK TO BASICS

DINOSAURS

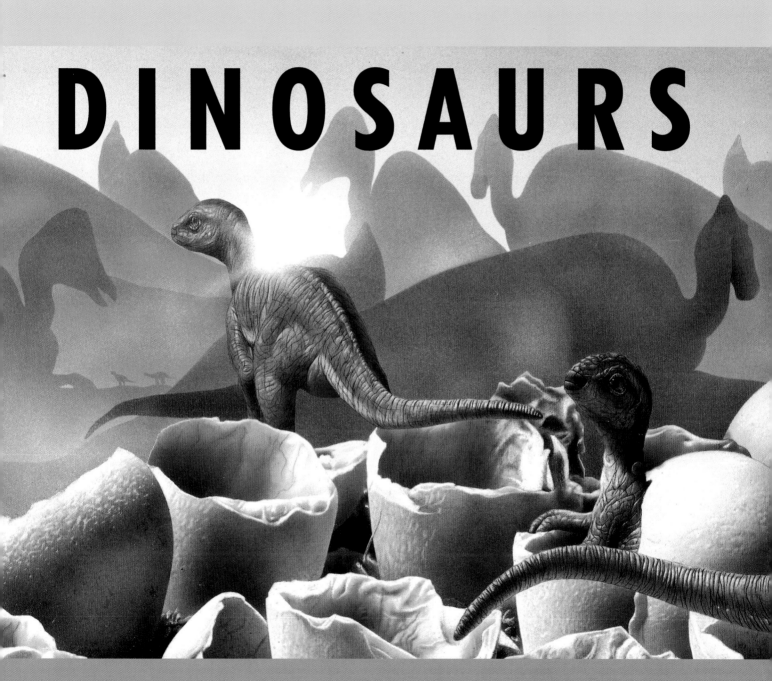

McRAE BOOKS

The dinosaur family tree

Early dinosaurs evolved from a group of reptiles called archosaurs. They split into two main groups—the saurischians and the ornithischians. Each group had different features. The main difference between the two was the shape and structure of their hip bones (see page 6).

✳ **Dinosaurs of the Golden Age** see pages 14–15

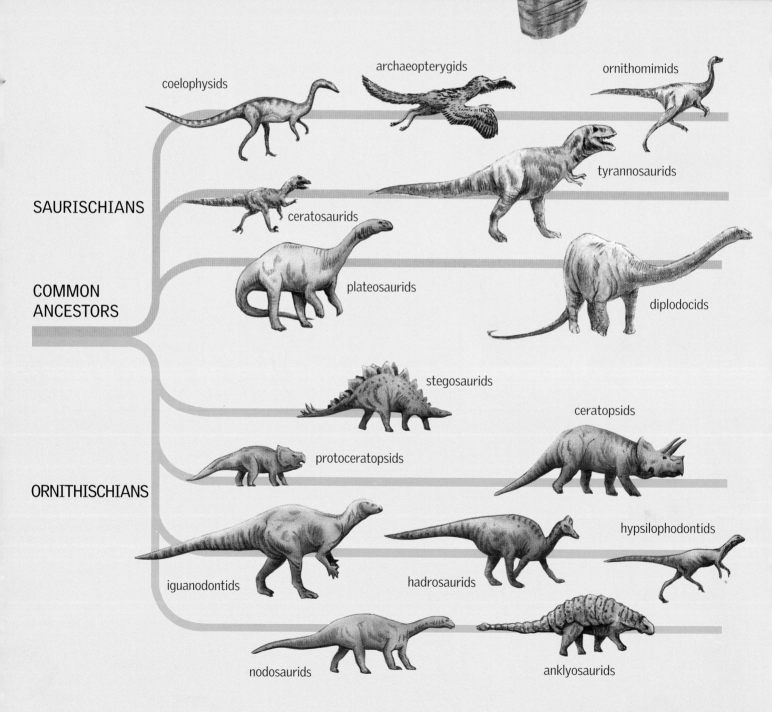

coelophysids

archaeopterygids

ornithomimids

tyrannosaurids

SAURISCHIANS

ceratosaurids

COMMON ANCESTORS

plateosaurids

diplodocids

stegosaurids

ceratopsids

protoceratopsids

ORNITHISCHIANS

hypsilophodontids

iguanodontids

hadrosaurids

nodosaurids

anklyosaurids

Weird and Wonderful
see pages 18–19

Lethal Hunters
see pages 16–17

Dinosaur Defense
see pages 22–23

Contents

What was a Dinosaur?	6–7	Dinosaur Defense	22–23
Before the Dinosaurs	8–9	Beneath the Waves	24–25
The First Dinosaurs	10–11	Up in the Air	26–27
Jurassic Giants	12–13	The End of the Dinosaurs	28–29
Dinosaurs of the Golden Age	14–15	Dinosaur Fun	30–31
Lethal Hunters	16–17	Index	32
Weird and Wonderful	18–19		
Dinosaur Babies	20–21		

Dinosaur Babies
see pages 20–21

Dinosaur Fun
see pages 30–31

Fossils

Fossils are the remains of plants or animals which have turned to stone over millions of years. The most common fossils are of hard parts, such as teeth, bones, and shells. Fossils have helped scientists to learn a great deal about dinosaurs.

Types of dinosaurs

The two main types of dinosaurs were the ornithischians and the saurischians. Ornithischian dinosaurs had hips like modern birds (see below top). Saurischian dinosaurs had hips like modern reptiles (see below bottom).

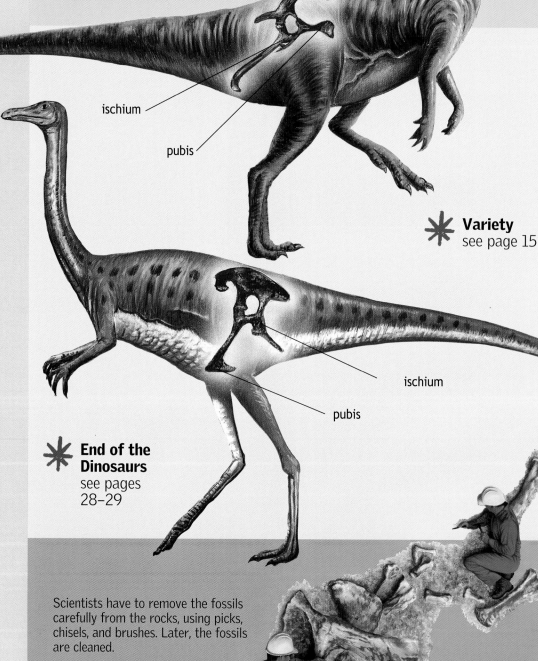

ischium

pubis

ischium

pubis

✳ **Variety**
see page 15

✳ **End of the Dinosaurs**
see pages 28–29

6

A dinosaur has died.

Its body gets covered with sediment.

The bones fossilize (turn into rock).

The fossil is uncovered by people or erosion.

Scientists have to remove the fossils carefully from the rocks, using picks, chisels, and brushes. Later, the fossils are cleaned.

Mealtimes

Some dinosaurs were carnivores (meat-eaters). They hunted other animals, including other dinosaurs. Other dinosaurs were herbivores (plant-eaters). Each type of dinosaur was well adapted to its lifestyle. Herbivores, for example, often had long necks to reach food high off the ground.

The largest carnivores were the tyrannosaurs. They had massive heads and jaws, lined with dagger-like teeth for ripping their prey apart. They hunted other dinosaurs.

The name "dinosaur" was first used by British scientist, Richard Owen (below), in 1842. In Greek, the word means "terrible lizard."

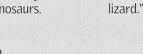

Hunters
see pages 16–17

What was a Dinosaur?

Dinosaurs were an extraordinary group of animals that lived on Earth from about 230–65 million years ago. They ranged in size from no bigger than modern chickens to giants over 100 feet (30 m) long. More than 500 species of dinosaurs have been discovered so far. Dinosaurs were reptiles with scaly skin and tough-shelled eggs, like modern reptiles. Unlike modern reptiles, however, some types of dinosaurs could also run and jump on their back legs.

Timeline

250–208 mya Triassic
First dinosaurs appear
First mammals appear

208–144 mya Jurassic
Dinosaurs dominate the Earth
Pterosaurs (flying reptiles) appear

144–65 mya Cretaceous
First flowering plants appear
First true birds appear
Dinosaurs become extinct

Habitat

Dinosaurs lived on land and their remains have been found all over the world. One of the richest sites for dinosaur hunters is the USA. But exciting discoveries have been made in every continent, including Antarctica, and finds are still being made.

Plateosaurus was a plant-eater that lived in Europe around 200 million years ago when the climate was hot and desert-like.

Life begins

The first living things on Earth were single-celled organisms called blue-green algae. They were not plants but were followed, about 1 billion years ago, by plants called true algae. The first animals were also single-celled and were called protozoans.

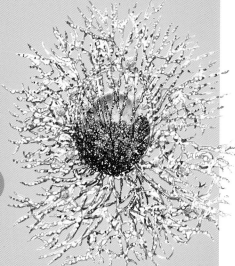

The first organisms on Earth were probably very like this modern single-celled protozoan.

This jawless fish lived in Australia about 500 million years ago.

Jolly jelly

Jellyfish still live in the sea today, as they did millions of years ago. They have soft, jelly-like bodies and tentacles equipped with stinging cells.

By grooming mammals form special bonds with others in their group. By grooming mammals form special bonds with others in their group.

8

Before
the Dinosaurs

For over 150 million years the dinosaurs were the largest and most important animals on Earth. But many other kinds of animals lived before the dinosaurs, including other types of reptiles. Long before animals, however, the first life on Earth appeared in the seas. Fossils of tiny cells have been found which are over 3.2 billion years old. The first animals also appeared in the sea, some 700 million years ago.

A bit of backbone

Early fish were among the first vertebrates (animals with backbones). They appeared about 500 million years ago. They were agnathans, which means "jawless." They filtered their food from the water, rather than biting or chewing it.

Amphibians evolved from fish, such as this Eusthenopteron. It used its fins to move on land.

Onto the land

The first vertebrates to move on to the land were amphibians. One of the earliest was called Ichthyostega. Its fossils were discovered in Greenland in rocks about 370 million years old. It had gills and lungs for breathing in the water and on land.

Dinosaur ancestors

The dinosaurs evolved from one group of reptiles, called archosaurs. Archosaurs were also the ancestors of modern-day birds and crocodiles. An early archosaur was Erythrosuchus (see right), one of the largest land predators of its time.

Erythrosuchus grew about 15 feet (4.5 m) long and lived about 230 million years ago in Africa.

Dimetrodon was a hunting reptile that lived in North America about 270 million years ago. It grew about 7 feet (2 m) long. It had a large sail of skin on its back, supported by bones. The sail may absorbed heat from the sun to help the animal warm up quickly.

Rise of reptiles

Reptiles evolved from amphibians but were better suited to life on land. Amphibians had to return to the water to lay their jelly-like eggs, otherwise they would have dried out. But reptiles laid hard-shelled eggs on land. Reptiles also had better limbs for walking.

Early hunters

The therapods were built for hunting. They could stand almost upright and run on their two rear legs. They had light-weight bodies for moving fast. As they ran, they held out their long tails for balance. Their claws were long and sharp for grabbing prey. Their powerful jaws were filled with sharp, curved teeth for tearing prey into pieces.

Coelophysis was a therapod that lived in North America. Built for speed, it had a light, slender body and long legs and tail. Its narrow jaws were lined with sharp, serrated teeth for attacking prey. It could dart its long neck from side to side.

Herrerasaurus was one of the larger therapods, built to hunt and kill fairly large prey. Sliding joints made its jaw extra-flexible for biting, and powerful muscles closed its mouth with a snap. It lived in South America and grew some 13 feet (3 m) long.

10

Prosauropods

The prosauropods were a group of large, long-necked dinosaurs that evolved to feed on plants. These dinosaurs walked on all fours but some could rear up on their back legs to reach the leaves of tall trees. Prosauropods may have first appeared in Africa about 210 million years ago but they spread quickly. Their fossils have been found on almost every continent.

Riojasaurus (right) was one of the biggest prosauropods. It grew about 30 feet (10 m) long and had a large, bulky body on strong, stocky legs. It was probably too heavy to walk on two legs. It may have traveled in herds as protection against hunters.

The First
Dinosaurs

During the middle of the Triassic Period (250-208 million years ago), the archosaurs split into three different reptile groups. The first were the ancestors of modern-day alligators and crocodiles. The second were the pterosaurs (flying reptiles). The third were the dinosaurs. The first dinosaurs were the saurischians (see page 6). They divided into two groups—the meat-eating therapods and the plant-eating prosauropods.

Postosuchus (below) was related to the ancestors of modern-day crocodiles. It grew about 20 feet (6 m) long and its body was covered in tough armor-plating. Its narrow jaws were armed with rows of lethal, dagger-like teeth.

Not all early dinosaurs were large. Eoraptor (skull shown right) was only about 3 feet (1 m) long and had a small, lightly-built body for fast running. Its fossils have been found in Argentina where it hunted in the prehistoric forests.

Competition

During the early days of the dinosaurs, many different creatures competed for food. One of the fiercest hunters of the time was a reptile called Postosuchus (right). It could rear up on its back legs to attack its prey.

12 Brachiosaurus (right) lived 150 million years ago in Africa and North America. It used its long neck to browse for food in the treetops, like a modern-day giraffe.

Body design

Sauropods had massive bodies with long necks and tails. To support this great weight, their legs were like huge, strong, solid pillars of bone. Sauropods had to be able to find and digest enough food to keep such a huge body going. Among their body features was a broad, deep rib cage which allowed room for a large stomach and intestines.

Digestion aids

To help them digest their bulky plant food, sauropods swallowed large numbers of stones or pebbles (above). These stones stayed in their stomachs, helping to mash the food into pulp so that it was easier to digest.

Defense

The sheer size of an adult sauropod was enough to keep attackers away. But sauropods had other means of Defense. Some may have used their large front claws to fight. Others swung their long tails at their enemies.

A sauropod's feet were wide and strong to carry its massive body weight. Many sauropods had a large, sharp claw on their front feet (see below).

Size

Among the largest animals that have ever lived, the sauropods were Jurassic giants. Brachiosaurus may have grown to about 75 feet (23 m) long and weighed 80 tons—as much as 12 African elephants! Diplodocus grew to about the same length but was much lighter at 11 tons because its backbones were partly hollow.

Jurassic
Giants

The first dinosaurs appeared during the Triassic Period. But it was really during the Jurassic Period (208–144 million years ago) that they came into their own. As the Earth's climate grew warmer and wetter, plant life flourished in regions which had been dry. With vast amounts of food available, plant-eating dinosaurs grew to an enormous size. The largest were the sauropods which included some of the biggest animals ever to live on land.

Food

The sauropods ate plants, such as tree ferns, cycads, and conifer trees. Some may have specialized in eating certain plants. For example, Diplodocus had comb-like teeth which may have been used for stripping off pine needles.

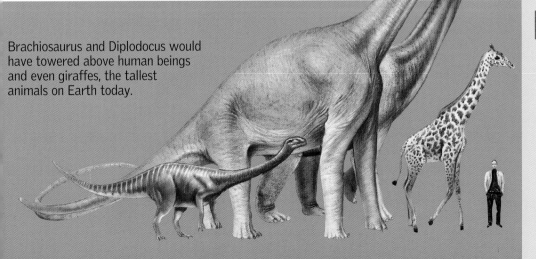

Brachiosaurus and Diplodocus would have towered above human beings and even giraffes, the tallest animals on Earth today.

Terror on land

Fearsome meat-eating dinosaurs ruled the Earth during the Cretaceous Period. Many ate large plant-eating dinosaurs. Others fed on fish and small mammals. They used razor-sharp teeth and terrible claws to catch and kill their victims.

14

The most feared hunter was Tyrannosaurus Rex. Its jaws were so strong that it could bite straight through bones.

Kronosaurus was probably the largest marine reptile that ever lived.

Many flying reptiles sailed through the skies during this period.

Hadrosaurs were also known as duck-billed dinosaurs.

Colors

Some dinosaurs may have attracted mates using displays of color. Many hadrosaurs had large crests on their heads. These may have been covered in brightly colored skin which would have been used to create a striking courtship display.

Calling

Some of the dinosaurs may have used calls to attract a mate. Muttaburrasaurus (below) had a bony bump on its nose. Blowing into the bump may have helped to create a loud, booming sound.

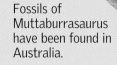

Fossils of Muttaburrasaurus have been found in Australia.

Dinosaurs of the
Golden Age

The Cretaceous Period (144–65 million years ago) was a golden age for the dinosaurs. The climate was warm and humid. About 140 million years ago, flowering plants appeared on Earth for the first time. Many new species of dinosaurs evolved to take advantage of these new sources of food. At the same time, some dinosaurs groups, such as the sauropods, died out as the new plant-eating dinosaurs took over their food supplies.

Variety

A wide range of dinosaurs appeared during the Cretaceous Period, including the hadrosaurs and the terrible tyrannosaurs. This growth in number and variety was most likely due to the spread of the first flowering plants. Many other new animals also appeared on Earth. They included new types of insects, such as bees and butterflies, and the first snakes.

Centrosaurus had a large neck frill and a long horn on its snout.

Spinosaurus was a hunter with a large sail running down its back.

Dromaeosaurus killed its prey with its large, curved claws.

Avimius, which means "bird mimic" was a small, fast dinosaur that lived at the end of the Cretaceous.

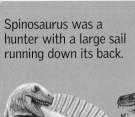

Fit for the hunt

Meat-eating dinosaurs shared a similar body plan, designed for a hunting lifestyle. Their back legs were longer for running after prey. Their shorter front limbs ended in hands equipped with sharp claws. Their heads were relatively large with powerful jaws.

This food pyramid shows how the dinosaurs were linked by what they ate. Large carnivores ate smaller carnivores and herbivores. Herbivores ate only plants.

In packs

Some of the smaller dinosaurs, such as Compsognathus (below), may have hunted in packs. Quick and agile, Compsognathus was only about the size of a modern-day chicken, making it one of the smallest dinosaurs known. Lizards and mammals were probably its main prey. The remains of a lizard have been found in a fossilized Compsognathus skeleton.

Deinonychus was a fast, nimble hunter, with a deadly claw on each of its feet. It used these lethal weapons for slashing into its victim's flesh.

Lean and mean

Some of the smaller, speedier dinosaurs were the best hunters. Velociraptor (right) could run at speeds of over 30 mph (50 km/h), holding its stiff tail out for balance. Its jaws were lined with about 80 very sharp, curved teeth and it had slashing claws on each foot.

A Velociraptor running after its prey.

This fearsome toe claw (left) belonged to Megaraptor. It measured an awesome 11 inches (27 cm) long.

Lethal
Hunters

The most feared dinosaurs of the Jurassic and Cretaceous were the meat-eating predators. Some were powerfully-built killers, capable of attacking the giant plant-eaters. Others were quick and small, and hunted lizards and mammals. A few lived by scavenging. They ate dinosaurs that had been killed or had died of natural causes. These deadly dinosaurs were well equipped with fearsome teeth and claws for killing prey and ripping up flesh.

Like many hunters, Allosaurus could open then slam its jaws with enough force to kill its prey.

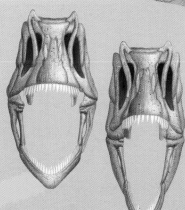

Open wide!

The most important hunting weapons were jaws lined with long, sharply pointed teeth. The edges of the teeth were jagged for tearing through flesh.

Bone Heads

Some dinosaurs, such as Pachycephalosaurus (right), had large, bony domes on top of their skulls. These domes probably acted as crash helmets to protect the dinosaurs' heads when they took part in head-butting contests with rival males.

A small bone-headed dinosaur, Stegoceras had a skull covered in bony knobs and lumps.

The bony dome on top of Pachycephalosaurus's head may have been up to 10 inches (25 cm) thick.

Oviraptor used its strangely shaped beak for cracking open dinosaur eggs.

Beaks

Different groups of dinosaurs developed different shapes of mouth and teeth to deal with the various types of food they ate. Some dinosaurs had sharp, parrot-like beaks. These were particularly efficient for feeding on plants and cracking open eggs.

Weird and Wonderful

During the late Cretaceous Period, many new groups of dinosaurs evolved. Some of these dinosaurs boasted extraordinary headgear, from horns and beaks, to crests and frills. One group of plant-eating dinosaurs, the ceratopsians, grew enormous frills of bones from the backs of their skulls. These may have been used for attracting mates, and for signaling to other ceratopsians. The ceratopsians also grew large horns as weapons against predators.

Crests

Some hadrosaurs (duck-billed dinosaurs), such as Parasaurolophus (left), had strangely shaped crests on the top of their heads. The crests were hollow and may have been used to make the dinosaur's booming calls louder.

Parasaurolophus's amazing backward-pointing crest was nearly 6 feet (2 m) long. It may have been brightly colored.

Horns

The ceratopsid dinosaurs had heads topped with sharp beaks, spectacular neck-frills, and large horns. This made their heads very heavy. The first three vertebrae (backbones) behind their heads were fused together into a solid piece of bone. This strengthened the tops of their necks to support the weight. The ceratopsids probably used their neck-frills for signaling and their horns for fighting with rivals and for self Defense.

Torosaurus had one of the largest skulls of any known animal. Including the neck frill, its skull measured more than 8 feet (2.5 m).

Triceratops may have used its three horns in fights with rival males and to protect itself from predators.

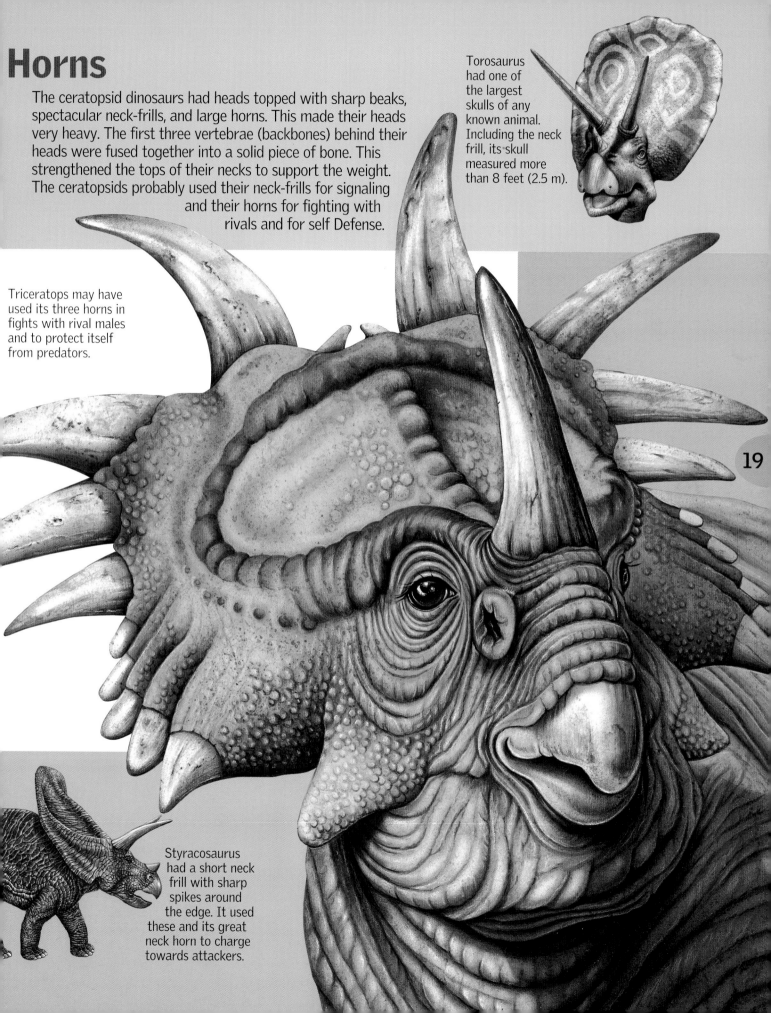

Styracosaurus had a short neck frill with sharp spikes around the edge. It used these and its great neck horn to charge towards attackers.

Fossil baby

Many fossilized dinosaur eggs have been found at sites all around the world. The eggs, which look like piles of stones, have been buried for millions of years. Newly-hatched dinosaurs, nests, and even embryos still inside their eggs have also been found.

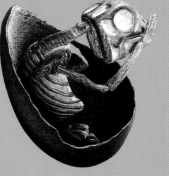

A fossil showing a dinosaur baby hatching out of its eggs.

Nourishing food

Dinosaur eggs made a nourishing meal for mammals and other dinosaurs, such as Oviraptor. Mother dinosaurs had to guard their nests and eggs against predators. Some dinosaurs built their nests in groups for extra protection.

An early rodent-like mammal eating a dinosaur egg.

Dinosaur
Babies

20

A clutch of Therizinosaurus eggs laid between 110–65 million years ago.

Many fossils of dinosaur eggs have been found, so we know that they had hard shells. The eggs also seem to show that certain types of dinosaurs were good parents and looked after their eggs and young. Some built nests for their eggs. Many covered the eggs with leaves or sand to keep them warm until they hatched.

Eggs

A dinosaur's egg had a tough, waterproof shell to protect the embryo (developing baby). Inside was a yolk that held food for the embryo. Some dinosaur eggs were as big as 5 inches (18 cm) long but others were much smaller. Some large dinosaurs hatched from small eggs.

A hadrosaur nest with eggs beginning to hatch.

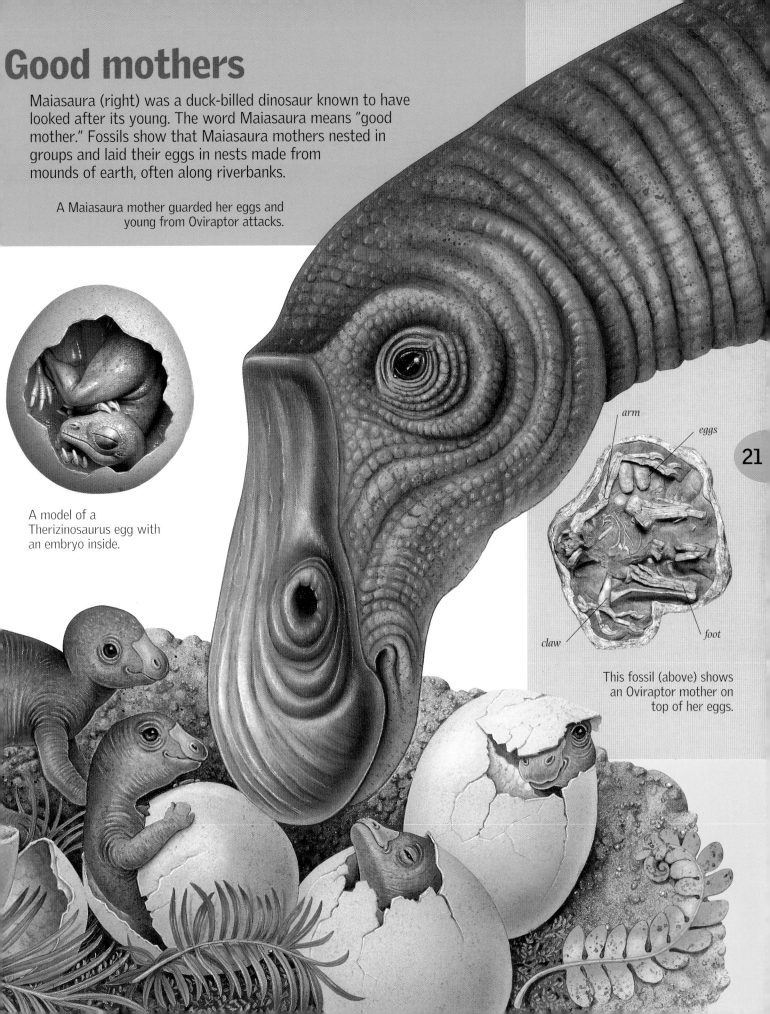

Good mothers

Maiasaura (right) was a duck-billed dinosaur known to have looked after its young. The word Maiasaura means "good mother." Fossils show that Maiasaura mothers nested in groups and laid their eggs in nests made from mounds of earth, often along riverbanks.

A Maiasaura mother guarded her eggs and young from Oviraptor attacks.

A model of a Therizinosaurus egg with an embryo inside.

arm

eggs

21

claw

foot

This fossil (above) shows an Oviraptor mother on top of her eggs.

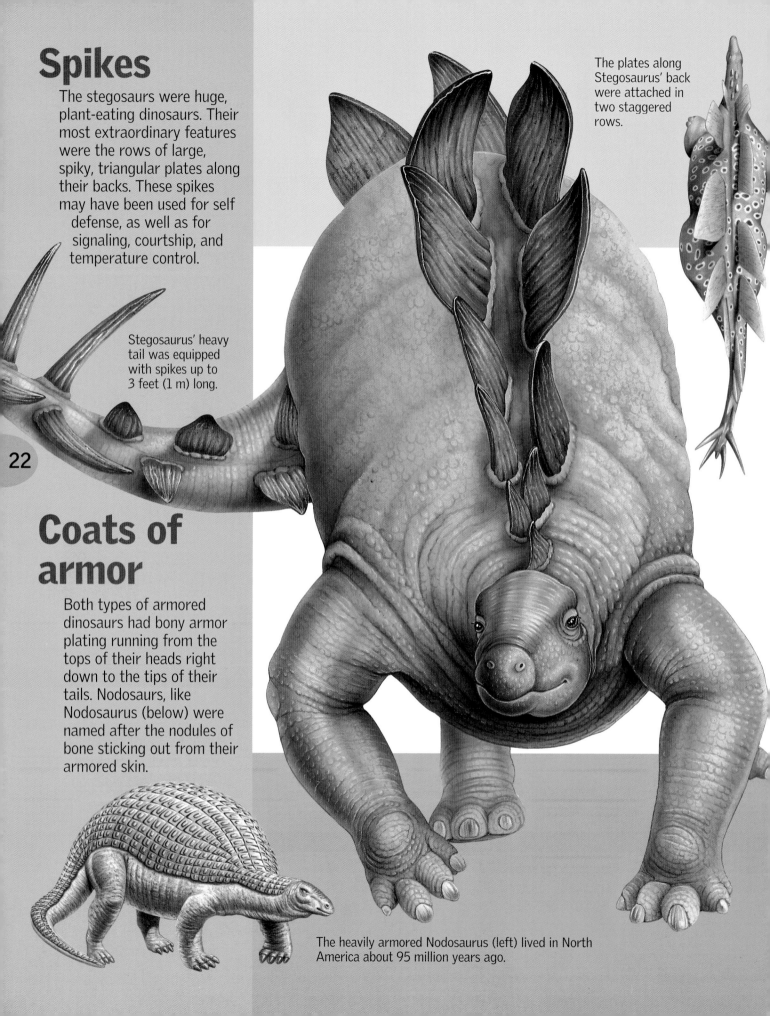

Spikes

The stegosaurs were huge, plant-eating dinosaurs. Their most extraordinary features were the rows of large, spiky, triangular plates along their backs. These spikes may have been used for self defense, as well as for signaling, courtship, and temperature control.

Stegosaurus' heavy tail was equipped with spikes up to 3 feet (1 m) long.

The plates along Stegosaurus' back were attached in two staggered rows.

22

Coats of armor

Both types of armored dinosaurs had bony armor plating running from the tops of their heads right down to the tips of their tails. Nodosaurs, like Nodosaurus (below) were named after the nodules of bone sticking out from their armored skin.

The heavily armored Nodosaurus (left) lived in North America about 95 million years ago.

Tail clubs

Ankylosaurs had a heavy ball of bone, like a club, at the end of their tails. If attacked, an ankylosaur used its tail as a weapon. It probably turned its back and swung its massive tail from side to side, causing serious damage to its attacker.

A view of an Ankylosaurus tail, showing its twin tail clubs.

A Euoplocephalus tail, seen from above.

A Euoplocephalus tail, seen from the side.

Dinosaur
Defense

Two groups of armor-plated dinosaurs were common in the Cretaceous Period. These were the nodosaurs and the ankylosaurs. Both had necks, backs, sides, and tails covered in thick plates of bone set into their leathery skin. Some of them also had spikes and clubbed tails. They used their armor, spikes, and tails to defend themselves against attack from hunting predators.

An ankylosaurid swinging its tail to protect itself from a hungry predator.

In action

Other species of dinosaurs had different ways of defending themselves from danger. When threatened, a group of Chasmosaurus huddled together. The largest dinosaurs stood on the outside, facing the enemy and waving their horns and crests.

Long necks

Long-necked reptiles called plesiosaurs swam in the seas throughout the Jurassic and Cretaceous Periods. They probably fed on fish, moving their long necks around in the water to grab their prey. The longest plesiosaur was Elasmosaurus (below).

Elasmosaurus's neck measured about 25 feet (8 m), more than half its overall body length. Its jaws were lined with sharp pointed teeth.

New fish

Many new types of fish also appeared in the Triassic seas. Among them were sharks, such as Hybodus (left). It was a fast-swimming, stream-lined hunter, like a modern shark.

Hybodus preyed on other fish, shrimps and crabs.

Beneath the Waves

24

Archelon (below) was a gigantic sea turtle which grew about 13 feet (4 m) long.

While the dinosaurs ruled the land, several groups of reptiles lived in the sea. As some species became extinct over millions of years, other new species appeared. Among the early marine reptiles were the nothosaurs. They died out by the end of the Triassic Period, when their place was taken by the plesiosaurs (left). Another large group of marine reptiles were the fish-like ichthyosaurs (right).

Surf and turf

Some reptiles lived in and around rivers, lakes, and the sea. Among them were turtles and crocodiles which first appeared in the Triassic Period. The first crocodiles were lightly built with long legs but, by the Jurassic, they looked remarkably like modern-day crocodiles. The largest crocodile that has ever lived was the Deinosuchus. It grew about 50 feet (15 m) long and probably lived on the banks of rivers where it preyed on dinosaurs.

Deinosuchus (left) lived in North America in the late Cretaceous Period.

Fast swimmers

With their streamlined bodies and powered by tails that beat from side to side, ichthyosaurs were the reptiles best suited to a marine life. But plesiosaurs and their relations, the pliosaurs, were also strong swimmers, using their large flippers to propel themselves along.

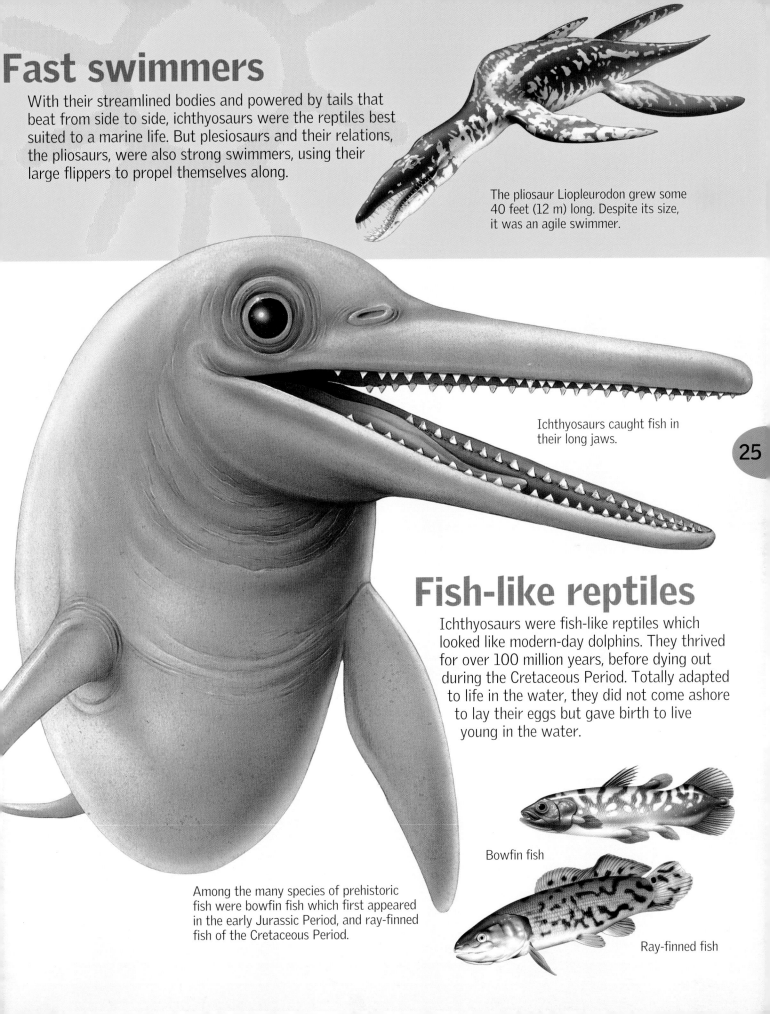

The pliosaur Liopleurodon grew some 40 feet (12 m) long. Despite its size, it was an agile swimmer.

Ichthyosaurs caught fish in their long jaws.

Fish-like reptiles

Ichthyosaurs were fish-like reptiles which looked like modern-day dolphins. They thrived for over 100 million years, before dying out during the Cretaceous Period. Totally adapted to life in the water, they did not come ashore to lay their eggs but gave birth to live young in the water.

Bowfin fish

Among the many species of prehistoric fish were bowfin fish which first appeared in the early Jurassic Period, and ray-finned fish of the Cretaceous Period.

Ray-finned fish

Long tails

Early pterosaurs, like Preondactylus (below) had long, bony tails which they used for balance as they flew. A diamond-shaped flap at the end may have acted like a rudder so that the pterosaur could steer.

Dimorphodon (below) was one of the earliest pterosaurs. It lived in Europe at the beginning of the Jurassic Period.

Wing span

During the Cretaceous Period, the short-tailed pterosaurs, or pterodactyls, grew to an enormous size. Quetzalcoaltus is thought to have had a 40-foot (12-m) wingspan, making it probably the biggest flying animal that has ever lived.

Tropeognathus (above) had a wingspan of about 20 feet (6 m).

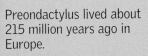
Preondactylus lived about 215 million years ago in Europe.

Winged reptiles

The word pterosaur means "winged-reptile". Pterosaurs were able to flap their wings to stay airborne and could also glide through the sky. Flying allowed them to hunt for food in the air and escape quickly from enemies.

Kuehneosaurus (above) was one of the first reptiles to take to the air. It did not fly but glided.

Germandactylus may have used its bony crest for signaling.

Up in the Air

Sharovipteryx was another early reptile that glided through the air.

During the time of the dinosaurs, other reptiles took to the air. The first flying reptiles were the pterosaurs. They appeared in the late Triassic Period and ruled the skies for millions of years. Pterosaurs had wings attached to the sides of their bodies and to the long fourth fingers on each of their hands. Early pterosaurs had long tails and short necks. Later pterosaurs, the pterodactyls, had shorter tails and longer necks.

Quick bite

From fossils of pterosaur jaws and teeth, scientists have been able to work out what pterosaurs ate. Some pterosaurs had long, pointed teeth for catching slippery fish from seas and lakes. They swooped low over the water, then snatched up fish in their jaws. Other pterosaurs had shorter, sharper teeth for catching their insect prey as they flew.

Anurognathus probably ate insects that it caught in mid-air.

Dorygnathus hunted for fish off the coasts of North America and Europe.

Effects

The catastrophic effects of the meteorite impact would have been felt far and wide. Some of these effects are shown below. The Earth's climate would have changed, devastating life both on land and in the sea.

Earthquakes

Tsunamis

Forest fires

Ash and dust

Acid rain

Climate change

Meteorite

Some experts believe that the reason for the dinosaurs' extinction was that a giant lump of space rock called a meteorite hit the Earth. This may have thrown up clouds of debris which blotted out the sun. First the plants died, then the plant-eating dinosaurs, then the carnivores.

Some experts believe that the meteorite hit the Yucatan Peninsula in Mexico.

The End
of the Dinosaurs

For about 165 million years, the dinosaurs were the most important animals on Earth. Then, about 65 million years ago, they and many other creatures became extinct. No one knows exactly what happened to the dinosaurs. Scientists have many different ideas. It may have been the result of one dramatic disaster, or a combination of several different disasters.

A volcanic eruption may have been to blame.

Volcano

Some experts think that a huge volcanic eruption caused the death of the dinosaurs. This could have thrown huge clouds of ash and dust into the air, causing the climate to change and killing plants and animals.

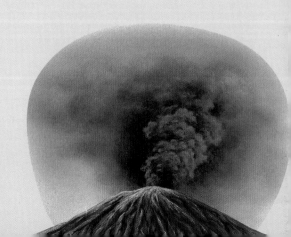

Moths need clean air to live and would not have survived a giant dust cloud. But they did not die out.

Other theories

There are many arguments against the meteorite theory. For example there are signs that its effects were not as wide-spread as first thought. There are also many other theories about why the dinosaurs died out.

Many animal species did survive, including mammals such as Alphadon (left).

The impact of a meteorite would have been devastating.

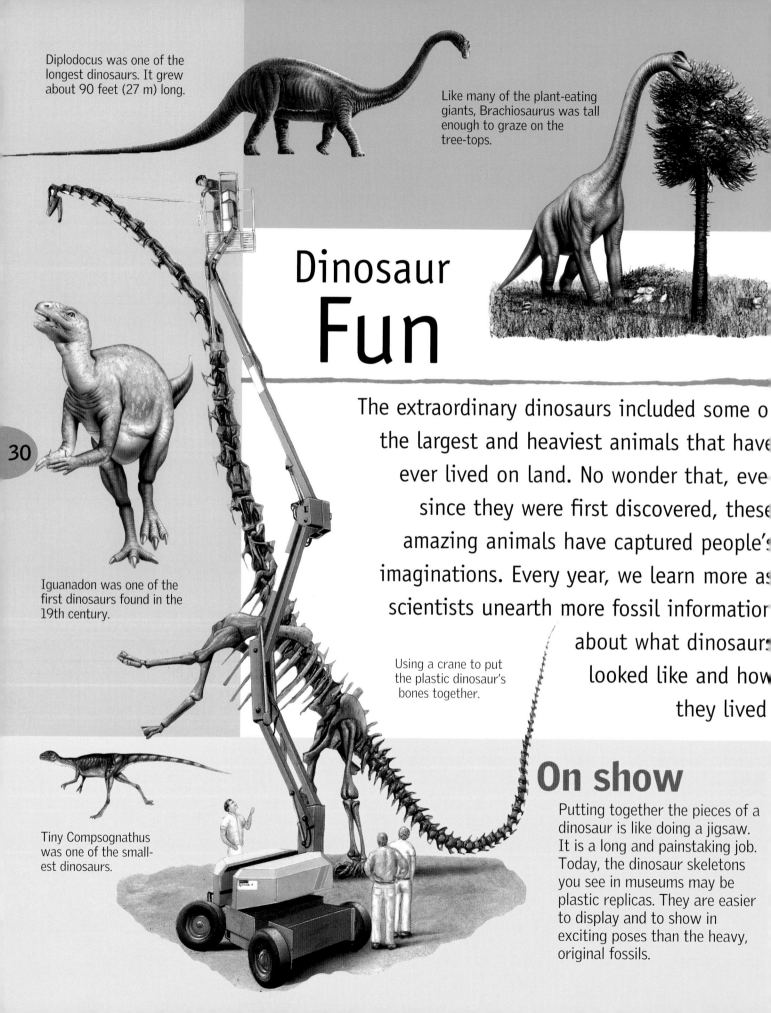

Diplodocus was one of the longest dinosaurs. It grew about 90 feet (27 m) long.

Like many of the plant-eating giants, Brachiosaurus was tall enough to graze on the tree-tops.

Dinosaur
Fun

Iguanadon was one of the first dinosaurs found in the 19th century.

Using a crane to put the plastic dinosaur's bones together.

Tiny Compsognathus was one of the smallest dinosaurs.

The extraordinary dinosaurs included some of the largest and heaviest animals that have ever lived on land. No wonder that, ever since they were first discovered, these amazing animals have captured people's imaginations. Every year, we learn more as scientists unearth more fossil information about what dinosaurs looked like and how they lived

On show

Putting together the pieces of a dinosaur is like doing a jigsaw. It is a long and painstaking job. Today, the dinosaur skeletons you see in museums may be plastic replicas. They are easier to display and to show in exciting poses than the heavy, original fossils.

Knowledge

Scientists are always looking for new ways to find out more about dinosaurs. In the film, Jurassic Park, scientists recreate a dinosaur by using the DNA from dinosaur blood found in a mosquito preserved in amber. In reality, this would be impossible.

An insect preserved in amber (fossilized tree sap).

Birds

Birds first appeared on Earth about 150 million years ago. It is thought that, over millions of years, a group of small, meat-eating dinosaurs started to grow feathers. Slowly, their arms became wings and they evolved into the first birds.

Modern birds are dinosaur descendants.

Film-makers use plastic models and computer-generated animation to bring the dinosaurs to life.

In the movies

Today, people are fascinated by dinosaurs even though they died out so long ago. Hundreds of books have been written about dinosaurs, and dinosaurs feature in many television programs and films. Scientists work closely with the writers, TV producers, and film-makers on these projects.

Gigantosaurus was an enormous hunter, weighing around 8 tons.

Index

Africa 9, 11, 12
Alligators 11
Allosaurus 17
Alphadon 29
amphibians 8, 9
Ankylosaurids 4, 23
Ankylosaurs 23
Ankylosaurus 23
Anurognathus 27
Archaeopterygids 4
Archelon 24
Archosaurs 9, 11
Argentina 11
Australia 8
Avimius 15

birds 9, 31
bowfin fish 25
Brachiosaurus 12, 13, 30

Centrosaurus 15
Ceratopsians 18, 19
Ceratosaurids 4
Chasmosaurus 23
Coelophysids 4
Coelophysis 10
Compsognathus 16, 30
Cretaceous Period 9, 14, 15, 17, 18, 23,
    24, 25, 26
crocodiles 9, 11, 24

Deinonychus 16
Deinosuchus 24
Dimetrodon 9
Dimorphodon 26
Diplodocids 4
Diplodocus 13, 30
Dorygnathus 27
Dromaeosaurus 15

Elasmosaurus 24
Eoraptor 11
Erythrosuchus 9
Euoplocephalus 23
Europe 27
Eusthenopteron 8

fossils 8

Gigantosaurus 31
giraffes 13

Hadrosaur 20
Hadrosaurids 4
Hadrosaurs 15, 18
Herrerasaurus 10
Hybodus 24
Hypsilophodontids 6

Ichthyosaurs 24, 25
Ichthyostega 8
Iguanadon 30
Iguanodontids 4

jawless fish 8
Jurassic Park 31
Jurassic Period 9, 13, 17, 24, 25, 26

Kronosaurus 14
Kuehneosaurus 27

Liopleurodon 25
lizards 16

Maiasaura 21
mammals 16, 20
marine reptiles 24, 25
Megaraptor 17
Mexico 28
Muttaburrasaurus 15

Nodosaurids 4
Nodosaurs 22, 23
Nodosaurus 22
North America 9, 12, 22, 27
nothosaurs 24

Ornithischians 6, 8
Ornithomimids 4
Oviraptor 18, 20, 21
Owen, Richard 9

Pachycephalosaurus 18
Parasaurolophus 18
Plateosaurids 4
Plateosaurs 6
Plateosaurus 9
Plesiosaurs 24

Pliosaurs 24
Postosuchus 11
Preondactylus 26, 27
Prosauropods 11
Protoceratopsids 6
protozoans 8
Pterodactyls 26, 27
Pterosaurs 9, 11, 26, 27

Quetzalcoaltus 26

ray-finned fish 25
reptiles 20
Riojasaurus 11

Saurischians 6, 8, 11
Sauropods 12, 13, 15
sharks 24
Sharovipteryx 27
South America 10
Spinosaurus 15
Stegoceras 18
Stegosaurids 4
Stegosaurs 22
Stegosaurus 22
Styracosaurus 19

Therapods 10, 11
Therizinosaurus 20, 21
Torosaurus 19
Triassic Period 9, 11, 13, 24, 27
Triceratops 19
Tropeognathus 26
turtles 24
Tyrannosaurids 4
Tyrannosaurs 6, 9
Tyrannosaurus Rex 14

Velociraptor 17

Yucatan Peninsula 28